Solids, Liquids, Gases, and Plasma

BY **DAVID A. ADLER**

ILLUSTRATED BY **ANNA RAFF**

HOLIDAY HOUSE
NEW YORK

For Caroline and Martin —D. A. A.

For Jacque —A. R.

The publisher wishes to thank Dr. Albert Rigosi of the National Institute of Standards and Technology for his expert review of the text.

Text copyright © 2019 by David A. Adler
Illustrations copyright © 2019 Anna Raff
All Rights Reserved
HOLIDAY HOUSE is registered in the U.S. Patent and Trademark Office.
Printed and bound in March 2022 at Toppan Leefung, DongGuan, China.
The artwork was created with ink washes, assembled and colored digitally.
www.holidayhouse.com
First Edition
3 5 7 9 10 8 6 4

Library of Congress Cataloging-in-Publication Data

Names: Adler, David A., author.
Title: Solids, liquids, gases, and plasma / David A. Adler.
Description: First edition. | New York : Holiday House,
[2019] | Audience: Ages 7–10. | Audience: Grades 4 to 6.
Identifiers: LCCN 2018061378 | ISBN 9780823439621 (hardcover)
Subjects: LCSH: Matter—Properties—Juvenile literature.
Classification: LCC QC173.36.A395 2019 | DDC 530.4—dc23
LC record available at https://lccn.loc.gov/2018061378
ISBN: 978-0-8234-3962-1 (hardcover)
ISBN: 978-0-8234-4839-5 (paperback)

Matter is everywhere.

Matter is anything that takes up space, even the smallest space, and has some weight, even the smallest weight.

A rock is matter. It takes up space and has weight. Books, shoes, and footballs are matter too.

A chocolate bar can teach you about matter.

Take a small bite of a chocolate bar. Of course, it tastes like chocolate.

Then place the bar flat
on a table and smash it
with your fist. It breaks
into tiny pieces. Taste some
of those small bits of
chocolate. They taste
like chocolate too.

Matter is like that. It's made of tiny bits, and each bit has the same properties as the larger piece. The tiniest bits of matter that have the same properties as the whole are called **molecules**.

WATER MOLECULES

Each drop of water is made up of trillions and trillions of water molecules. Each water molecule is made of even smaller particles: **atoms**. An atom is the smallest bit of an **element**, one of more than one hundred known building blocks of our world. Iron, silver, gold, copper, oxygen, zinc, and hydrogen are all examples of elements.

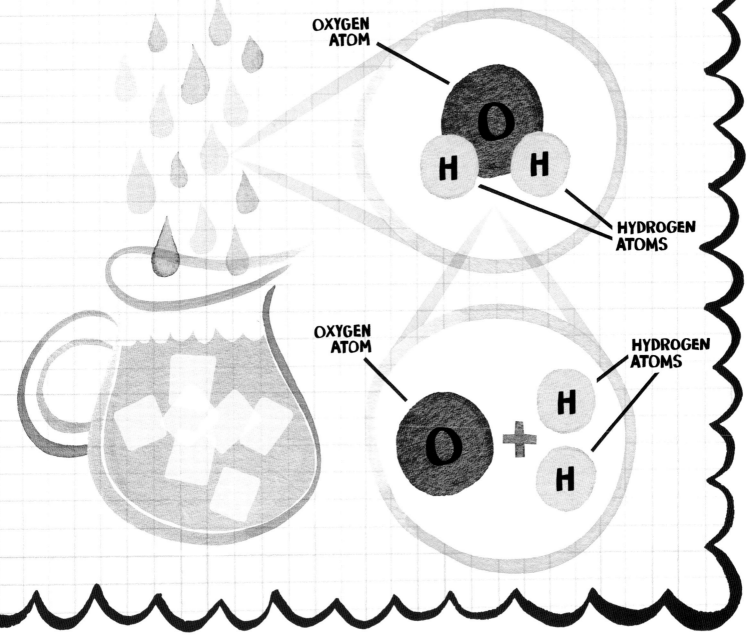

WATER MOLECULE

OXYGEN ATOM

HYDROGEN ATOMS

O

H   H

OXYGEN ATOM

HYDROGEN ATOMS

O + H

H

What happens when matter changes its form?

The molecules that make ice and other solids are bound together. They don't move.

8

The molecules that make water and other liquids are held together more loosely. They flow and move about.

The molecules that make water vapor and other gases are not held together at all.

Rocks, pebbles, books, shoes, and footballs are **solids**, a form of matter that has a definite shape.

Even a sheet of paper is a solid. Yes, you can fold it. You can cut it into many pieces. But if the sheet of paper is left alone, it will keep its shape.

Solids can be hard or soft. A golf ball is a solid. It's hard. A marshmallow is also a solid. It's soft.

The golf ball and the marshmallow might be about the same size. But they don't weigh the same. The golf ball is heavier than the marshmallow. It has a greater **density**. It packs more matter into the same amount of space.

Water, milk, juice, and other **liquids** take up space and have weight, so they are matter too. But liquids don't have a definite shape. They take the shape of their containers. You can prove this.

Fill a glass about halfway with water. The shape of the water in that glass is tall and cylinder-shaped.

Now pour the water into a flat, square pan. Now the water is flat and square-shaped.

Liquids take the shape of their containers.

Liquids are often measured by their **volume**, the amount of space they occupy. Liquids change shape when they are poured from one container to another, but their volume does not change. If you have two different-shaped measuring cups, you can prove it.

1. Pour enough water into one cup so it reaches exactly the half-cup mark.

2. Then pour from the first measuring cup to the other.

3. It may look like there's a different amount of water in the second cup, that the volume has changed, but it has not. In the second cup the water level should also reach exactly the half-cup mark.

Just like solids, liquids can take up the same amount of space, and have the same volume, but not weigh the same. To prove it, you'll need two liquids. Water and cooking oil would work. You'll also need two identical paper or plastic disposable cups, a ruler, a marker, and a postal or diet scale. If you don't have a scale, you can still do the experiment.

1. With the ruler, make a mark exactly one inch up on each cup.

2. Fill one cup to the line with water. Fill the other cup to the line with oil.

3. Now weigh each cup. The cup with oil weighs less than the cup with water. If you're not using a scale, pick up one cup in each hand. They each have the same volume, but they don't weigh the same. The cup with water should feel slightly heavier. This is because oil is less dense than water.

Gases are a third form of matter. Gases don't simply take the shape of their containers. They completely fill whatever container or space they're in.

Air is a mixture of gases. It fills every corner of every room in your home. But it's difficult to see the air. Smoke is also a mixture of gases, and it's easy to see smoke.

Imagine someone putting food in an oven and forgetting about it. The food would burn, and smoke would fill the room. There would be smoke everywhere.

Gases surely take up space. But to be a form of matter it must also have weight.

Gases have weight, and you can prove it.

You'll need a large deflated balloon and a postal scale.

Weigh the balloon.

Now, blow up the
balloon—fill it with air.
Weigh it again.
The balloon filled with
air will weigh more than it
did when it was deflated.
Air is a mixture of gases,
and it has weight.

Just like with solids and liquids, not all gases weigh the same. You can also learn this from balloons.

If you hold a balloon filled with air and let it go, without wind to blow it around, the balloon would fall to the ground. But if the balloon is filled with helium instead of air, it would float up. Air is a mixture of gases. Helium is a gas too, but it's lighter than air. That's why balloons filled with helium float.

Gases take up space and have weight. Gases are a form of matter.

Matter can change from one form to another, from solid to liquid and from liquid to gas.

SOLID

Ice is the solid form of water. When ice is exposed to heat, it changes from a solid to a liquid—it changes to water.

LIQUID → GAS

When a pot of water is put on a hot stove, the water boils. Steam rises above the pot. That steam is water **vapor**, a gas. When water is exposed to enough heat, it turns to water vapor.

Most matter can change states. But for many it takes extreme temperatures to change from solid to liquid to gas.

212 °F — 100 °C

32 °F — 0 °C

Ice will melt—change to water—when the temperature rises to just above 32 degrees Fahrenheit (just above 0 degrees Celsius). Water changes to vapor at 212 degrees Fahrenheit (100 degrees Celsius).

5,400 °F — **2,970°C**

4,480 °F — **2,470°C**

1,950 °F — **1,060°C**

1,220 °F — **660°C**

FANCY FOIL

For aluminum to melt—change to a liquid—it must be just over 1,220 degrees Fahrenheit (about 660 degrees Celsius). Its liquid form will change to vapor at about 4,480 degrees Fahrenheit (about 2,470 degrees Celsius).

Gold will melt at 1,950 degrees Fahrenheit (about 1,060 degrees Celsius). Its liquid form will change to vapor at nearly 5,400 degrees Fahrenheit (2,970 degrees Celsius).

Plasma, sometimes called ionized gas, is the fourth form of matter. It's gas with an electric charge.

Plasma, like gas, does not have a set shape or volume. It fills its container.

Fluorescent and neon lights are tubes with gas inside. They are turned on when electricity passes through the tubes and the gas becomes glowing plasma. Most stars, including the sun, are great masses of plasma.

EARTH MATTERS

Look around your room.

Of course, since you are looking through air, you are looking *through* matter. And you are looking *at* matter because anything you can see is matter—anything that takes up space and has weight, whether it's a solid, liquid, gas, or plasma.

GLOSSARY

Atom—The smallest bit of any element

Density—The amount of matter in a certain space

Element—Matter made up of just one kind of atom

Gas—Matter with no set shape or volume

Liquid—Matter with no set shape

Matter—Anything that takes up space and has weight

Molecule—The smallest bit of anything, made of atoms of more than one element—
a molecule of water is made of atoms of hydrogen and oxygen

Plasma—Gas with an electrical charge

Solid—Matter with a definite shape

Volume—The amount of space something occupies

Vapor—Matter as a gas that is a liquid at room temperature